# RISING FROM THE ASHES

## A MONTH OF PRAYER TO HEAL OUR WOUNDS

## ADOLFO QUEZADA

**Resurrection Press**
**An Imprint of**
**CATHOLIC BOOK PUBLISHING CO.**
Totowa • New Jersey

# To Roberto

First published in February 2002 by Resurrection Press, Catholic Book Publishing Company.

Copyright © 2002 by Adolfo Quezada

ISBN 1-878718-72-X

Cover design by John Murello

Photo by Kathy Willens / Reuters / Pool / Timepix

Printed in Canada.

1 2 3 4 5 6 7 8 9

# Contents

# Foreword

The Christian meaning of death is revealed in the light of the Paschal mystery of the death and resurrection of Jesus Christ in whom resides our only hope. The emphasis is on Christian hope in eternal life and in the final resurrection from the dead. The tragic disasters of September 11, 2001, have moved Christians to reflect upon the Paschal mystery through a fresh and meaningful perspective.

Since September 11, we have seen evil at its worst and goodness at its best. Evil came in the form of unprovoked and merciless attacks at the World Trade Center, the Pentagon, and on a field in Pennsylvania. This resulted in nearly 3,000 deaths. Goodness has come in the form of a quick response by Americans to help those who were suffering. I have witnessed New Yorkers from all walks of life coming together in unprecedented unity and solidarity.

This horrible tragedy also spurred a tremendous increase of people attending their respective houses of worship, whether it be a church, mosque or synagogue. Is it the fear of death or is it the fear of God that moves people to a religious experience? Before, we used to say there are no atheists in foxholes. Now, we say there are no atheists at Ground Zero. America has been wounded by evil and is gradually being healed by prayer and communal support in its houses of worship.

Memory is the faculty by which a person preserves, reproduces and identifies his or her past experiences. Who can forget the sights of the collapse of the Twin Towers at the World

Trade Center? The destruction of the Pentagon? The sight of a crashed airplane in Pennsylvania due to the perceived heroic actions of passengers who possibly avoided the destruction of another hallowed national landmark? There are many memories and they need to be put in a spiritual perspective.

The memory is highlighted in all the Eucharistic prayers when the priest prays with the community, "Remember, Lord, those who have died and have gone before us marked with the sign of faith, especially those for whom we now pray." The Roman Catholic Church has always had a daily reminder of those who died and how precious they are to us still through our memories and the celebration of the Eucharist. Numerous funeral liturgies and memorial Masses have been celebrated since September 11 and are based on the words of Jesus, "Do this in remembrance of me." We bless the dead and give comfort to the living.

A living reminder of God's presence at Ground Zero is the steel-based cross discovered amidst the rubble of World Trade Center 6. The cross has been transferred on top of a concrete median within Ground Zero. For Christians, the cross symbolizes Jesus Christ as both Victim and Victor. Christ was a victim of senseless violence. He was betrayed, denied, and abandoned by his own apostles. Christ was a victim of an unfair trial and scourging along the way to Calvary.

However, Christ was a Victor. He was victorious over death through the Resurrection and fulfilled the promise of eternal life for all who believe and worship. America, like Christ, is also Victim and Victor. America was victimized by senseless terrorist attacks. America is also the Victor by pulling together as a united country to rebuild once again. America's cross represents our present suffering and our eventual victory over terrorism.

Adolfo Quezada's *Rising from the Ashes: A Month of Prayer to Heal Our Wounds* helps the reader to heal spiritually and to ask God to give us hope in our present crisis. His book epitomizes the spirit of Romans 8:18: "I consider the suffering of the present time as nothing compared to the glory to be revealed in us." America is struggling and this season of sorrow beckons us to consider the glory of God within us.

—*Fr. Brian Jordan, OFM*

Father Brian Jordan, OFM is a Franciscan priest. He has been ministering at Ground Zero since September 11, 2001.

# Preface

Even as we moved in ordinary time, the peace of our normalcy was shattered. The shadow of our humanity collided with the light, and our world would never be the same. On that September morning hatred and fear struck at the heart of America leaving death and destruction in its wake. Terrorists had flown hijacked commercial airliners into the World Trade Center towers in New York City and into the Pentagon in Washington, D.C. Another plane crashed in the countryside of Pennsylvania. Never before had the enemy of freedom penetrated so deeply the flesh of our being. Never had the fabric of our security been so rent. The gates of hell had opened and terror raised its ugly head. The fires tortured and then consumed, the foundations shuddered and then collapsed. The agony and desolation were beyond belief, the meaning of it all, beyond our grasp. Why must we endure the pain of a loveless world? Why are we being persecuted? And then, the second wave of torment: grieving losses and picking up the pieces that were left.

The storm was dark and the clouds of life loomed over us like giant shadows. We were afraid. This was the day we had hoped would never come. Our hearts were heavy. In the beginning of those dark times, we felt abandoned. We were victims of the attacker's hate, symbols of their enemy. They tried to separate, hurt, and humiliate us; they traipsed on our name and stole our life away. At times like these, we dare to stay and wait, clenching our hands together in a prayer of desperation.

*The night is too long to bear alone. God, where have you gone? Then we hear your voice, dear God, a friend in the middle of the night. You come, not with legions of angels to avenge our wounds, but as a sweet and gentle resonance deep within our soul. You do not take the pain away, you do not bring the dawn. Instead, you take your place with us in the darkness of our life. We believe, help our disbelief; we hope, help our hopelessness; we forgive, help our unwillingness to forgive.*

It is one thing to have faith when all is well in our life, and it is quite another to believe when everything has been torn from us, when our world has been turned upside down. *Rising From The Ashes* is about a faith in God who speaks to us in silence, who comes to us in darkness, and who follows us into hell itself to bring us back to where we belong. The essence of this book is the call to God-consciousness. When we are aware of the immanence of God, we enter into equanimity. The circumstances that confront us may be bright or may be dark, yet, in the depth of our existence there is hope and there is joy.

This book is about recognizing the presence of God, even in the worst circumstances. The tragic events of September 11 are an example of the darkness through which we must sometimes pass before we enter into light. There is a tragedy happening every day to someone, somewhere. Perhaps you have been devastated by a serious disease or illness. Perhaps your marriage is failing or your children are in trouble. It may be that you have suffered a tremendous loss and are in the midst of grief. Whatever it is that is burdening your soul, my hope is that these pages will offer you some solace and comfort. Even though the book has been formatted as a month of prayers, please feel free to read and reflect at your own pace.

To be touched by God does not mean that our sadness is gone. We still encounter times of grief and trouble. We still experience pain and sometimes doubt and confusion. But all of these do not break us because we face our days with the love of God; they do not overcome us because we use what God has given us to cope, adjust, and make the best of life. To live in God-consciousness does not make us eternally somber or fatalistically resigned to the suffering that comes in life. It means that, even in the midst of suffering, and despite our losses, our heart is joyful because we live in God.

Our faith is sustained in prayer. Through our meditation and communion with God, we open to the everlasting energy of love. From our faith we draw fortitude, strength, and courage. Our faith moves from passion to compassion. It empties us of that which does not matter, that we may be filled with that which does. We may not always understand the ways of God, but it is when we least understand, yet cling to God, that our faith is most intense.

*Faith is the substance of things hoped for, the evidence of things not seen.*                                                          *Hebrews 11:1*

Help me, God, to rebuild my house. Give me the courage to dismantle it brick by brick, plank by plank, so that I may start anew. This time let me build it on the foundation of your holy name. Now, as I build, let it be on the base of your constant love for me and for all humanity. Set deeply in the ground of faith, my house will stand against the strongest winds, the unexpected torrents, and the overwhelming floods. Anchored in the solidity of your everlasting presence, I can make it through the storm.

You, my God, are the rock of my eternity. You are all there is; all rests on you. When everything else seems unpredictable, your order will be there. When my life appears to crumble, your words will hold it together. When the whole world seems ugly and menacing, the beauty of your nature will prevail, and the assurance of your love will offer me respite. You, Beloved, are the bedrock of my life; I make you the cornerstone of all I build.

*Week I*

# DARK FAITH

*Acknowledging Our Loss*

*"I said to my soul, be still and let the dark come upon you, which shall be the darkness of God."*
—*T.S. Eliot*

# Day 1: Entering the Darkness

*. . . You had endowed me with majesty and strength.*
*But now when you hide your face, I am terrified.*
*(Ps 30:7)*

How can it be that one moment God fills our thoughts, shares in our emotions, and permeates our bones, while in the next we are reduced to nomads wandering in the desert alone, without purpose, direction, or understanding; children abandoned. Our prayers are like cries in the night, unheard, unanswered. There are people all around us, yet, we are alienated from them and from ourselves. The bird still sings and the sun still shines, but we do not relish the song or move in the light.

These are times when our faith is tested, times when we do not see or feel the presence of God, when the voice of God is silent, and the touch of God is distant. It is during these times of doubt that our enemies advance toward the fortress of our soul. Fear threatens our right flank, while despair charges at our left. We cry out, "My God, my God, why have you forsaken me?" (Mt 27:46).

Where is the foundation on which we used to stand securely? The feelings of joy and ecstasy in prayer are also gone. The desert through which we walk is dry.

*Such is the nature of our faith, dear God: to believe in you*
*in spite of the signs, to see your light through the darkness, and*
*to hear your song, even in the silence.*

# Day 2: Doubting and Despairing ❀

*Be constantly on watch! Stay awake! You do not
know when the appointed time will come.*

*(Mk 13:33)*

The sense of God's presence eludes us and we feel alone
and lost. In our desperation, we will turn to anything that may
fill this terrifying void. We pray harder and longer, we even
try new ways to pray. Maybe if we just make a stronger effort,
maybe if we just hit upon the right spiritual practice, maybe if
we search far enough for the key to the kingdom, we will be
allowed back in. But all is to no avail. We cannot manipulate
ourselves, the world, or God. Any meaning that we bring
about by force is meaningless. In this black time, the strength
of our soul abandons us. It seems the more we assert our power,
the more separated we become.

We wait into the night and God does not come. The flame
of our faith flickers and our resolve is on the wane. We are not
prepared to persevere. Our depression gives into sleep. We do
not know the hour of God's coming. In our panic we do not
prepare for the wait. From the midst of the darkness God
comes to take our hand, but in our slumber, we fail to respond.

*Why, dear God? Why does our heart keep beating to the
rhythm of your heart? Why does our soul march on as though it
were protected against all foe? Why is it that when everything
around us seems hopeless, we hope? Why is it that although we
find no evidence on which to place our faith, we believe?*

# ❋ Day 3: Confronting God as Darkness ❋

*Within a short time you will lose sight of me, but soon after that you shall see me again. (Jn 16:16)*

How helpless we are through this dark night. If only we could hurry the dawn and end this state of unknowing. But could it be that the purpose of this darkness is to enlighten? Could it be that the helplessness we feel is the first sign that we are ready to be helped?

Even as we pine for God, and our soul yet yearns for what was there, the spring returns with even more than what we thought was lost, and we come to understand: God has not left us after all. The presence we have come to know is not enough for us. It has to go away for just a little while so a deeper communion with God may come. Now we surrender to God; now we die that God may live.

*Now we are guided in truth, and the ways of heaven are revealed to us. Your voice, dear God, is heard at yet a deeper place, a quiet place, a restful place. We still know sadness and we still shed tears, yet through the grief you lift our heart and our sorrow turns to joy. The pain of birth is felt and then it goes away, but the joy of life remains forever.*

# Day 4: Waiting in the Darkness

*Sit in silence and go into darkness . . .*

*(Isaiah 47:5)*

The danger of the dark night is that it ends and light returns. The tragedy is that in the light of day we forget what we have learned. We are distracted from the presence of God. We revert back to our childish faith, and we separate from God and therefore from the world.

Stripped of all that we have depended on, including our own ability, we are left with nothing but faith. Now we simply wait upon God in loving attention and with a quiet heart. Now our soul rests and waits.

The God of love and mercy abides in us. As we await God's coming, we already feel the joy of God's seed deep within us. We are pregnant with God's spirit. God comes to us, not because we have earned God's presence through our own virtue, but because it is God's nature to love us with this intimacy. We do not attract God with our beauty, God comes because we belong to God.

God comes when we least expect it. Our readiness must be constant, our door always open. Let our hearts be ever ready to receive. Let us be found living and loving.

*Our soul yearns for your presence, dear God, and waits with great anticipation, while at the same time it rests in the belief that it already possesses and is possessed by you. In our love for you the eternal future merges with the living present.*

*Our soul waits for the Lord, he is our help and shield . . .                                                      (Psalm 33:20)*

When we are stripped of the externals that gratify us, we are left with the love of God. When we no longer can depend on the fruit, we come to know the Tree. The fringes of spirituality disappear, the good feelings and high sensations burn out. The haven to which we would run to escape the world has been gutted out. Now it is without the pleasure of prayer that we pray. It is in the midst of the world that we find our haven. It is without seeing that we believe.

The torment of our soul in these darkened times is that of perceived abandonment. Because we seek God in the light, we feel forsaken when darkness comes. But when we see God everywhere, including the darkness, we are not abandoned, even in the night.

We come to learn that the love that comes of God and returns to God is centered, not on feelings that come and go, but on the will which is constant and permanent. It is not within our power or human responsibility to generate spiritual movement. It is not for us to ensure the presence of God. Ours is but to make ourselves quietly available to God, even through the dark times.

*We enter into darkness, absence, and emptiness, and there we wait for you, God. You come because you are the creator of life, you come because you are the light of understanding, but most of all, you come because you are love and you cannot help but share yourself with your beloved.*

16

# Day 6: Letting God be God

*No one has ever seen God, but if we love one another God lives in us, and his love is perfected in us.*                    *(1 Jn 4:12)*

We allow God to be revealed to us in whatever way the Divine chooses to be known at this moment. When we let go of the God images on which we have built our faith, we free God from the prison of our conception, and liberate God from the chains of our shallow characterizations.

Our belief in God can no longer be contingent on the circumstances of our life, but on the belief in God's love that emanates from our deepest self. Our intention with God must now be stripped of everything except our love.

As we embrace our ignorance, we are enlightened; as we release our expectations, we are surprised. It is from our state of openness that we invite God to come to us, and it is because of our readiness that God is revealed.

Our communion with God is like the joining of precious metals. The fire must be sufficiently intense for the breakdown of entities and the melting together of elements. It is in the surrendering of whom we have imagined ourselves to be that we can melt into God's essence; and it is in the surrendering of the limited concepts that we have of God that we can recognize God in all that is.

*You, who have no name, are known to our heart. You, who have no face, are seen by our soul. You, who are silent, are heard in our silence. You, who are illusive, are with us forever.*

17

# Day 7: Touching God

*Beloved, let us love one another because love is
from God; everyone who loves is born of God and
knows God.                            (1 Jn 4:7)*

In the presence of God we taste the sweet wine of union
and become drunk with love. We enter a place in the soul we
have never been before. All is one and one is all. The boundaries of our ego fall away and we find ourselves relating to the
ants and the birds, the flowers and the trees. We are in them
and they are in us. We are separate and together, different and
the same.

Standing on this hallowed ground we can see the multi-
plicity of one, and the unity among the pieces. God has many
faces, yet, there is but one God. We feel related to every person. We feel empathetic, compassionate, and connected. There
grows in us a deep respect for others because we know we all
belong to the whole. It is as though we have ceased to exist as
a separate entity, yet, we are fully aware of our individuality. It
is a paradox filled with splendor. All of our plans and schemes
melt into one purpose: to let God love through us. All else
becomes superfluous, petty, and silly.

*It is a long and lonely winter, and we pray to you, God,
believing in your seed that is planted in the depths of our soul.
We wait and watch, expecting the promise of new life, filled
with the joy of your eternal presence.*

18

*Unknown God, I see you now. You are different than I expected. You come from nowhere and then disappear into nothingness. I cannot predict you; I dare not summate you. You are too free to be captured for the sake of my understanding. You are beyond the limits of my projection, and you transcend the boundaries of my imagination. You are God.*

*Unknown God, I can no longer find you in the sentimentalism of religion. It is not enough to meet you within the confines of a church or an image on a wall. You are so much more. You are not the good that opposes evil, you are the good that embraces all, even evil. You are not the force that saves me from the pain of living; you are the force that brings me life even in the midst of pain.*

*Unknown God, you, who know power beyond my comprehension, also know the sense of my powerlessness. You, who know the ecstasy of heaven, also know the agony of my hell. In your wildness you are everywhere, even where I least expect to find you. I want to find you on the mountaintop where you can show me beauty and truth, peace and glory, and surely you are there. Yet, I encounter you mostly in the valley where ugliness and falsehood abound, and conflict and darkness are a way of life. You are there because there is where you find me.*

*Unknown God, I no longer look to you for answers or solutions to my problems. I need only your light that I may use my problems to move me closer to you. I no longer ask that you give me what I want, but that I come to appreciate what you have already given me.*

*Unknown God, I find you in the jungle of my complicated life. You are in the forest where I become lost. As I drown in the ocean, I meet you at the depths. And you are in the desert where I am dry and desolate, where life seems nearly impossible. Unknown God, you are there and everywhere I am.*

*Week II*

# SILENCE AND SOLITUDE

*Surrendering to God*

*"For God alone my soul waits in silence . . ."*
                                                      *—Psalm 62:1*

# Day 1: Receiving and Releasing

*When Jesus heard this (that John the Baptist had been killed), he withdrew from there in a boat to a deserted place by himself.* (Mt 14:13)

It was the day my son was born. No words can describe the coming of my firstborn. I was in awe; I was in shock; I was in joy and expectation. I was afraid; I was excited; I was open to what would come. I walked until I found a place apart. Here, in the solitude that had to be, I said a grateful prayer and pledged responsibility. Here, away from all the people, I was alone with God. Only God, I believed, could understand this rapture.

Seventeen years later my son was killed and my world exploded into shambles. There was chaos; there was terror; there was confusion and disbelief. Above all, there was constant company. At the hospital, at the service, and for many days thereafter, people came with good intentions to offer comfort and condolence. This is how it is in times of loss. Community closes ranks in grand support and much good will. I accepted the gift of presence from all who came, and I was very grateful. But then there came a time to enter serious grieving and I had to go alone. There are moments in our life that we can share with God alone. Only God can know such agony, as only God can know the bliss.

*First we cry the tears of sorrow. We have loved and we have lost. The sun has left, the moon remains to mourn with us, to spend the night remembering. Then comes your dawn, dear God, the light breaks through, and the morning brings the healing.*

## ❀ Day 2: Entering the Desert of the Heart ❀

*I will lead her into the desert, and there I will speak to her heart.* *(Hosea 2:16)*

Sometimes when we are alone, especially if we allow meditation and prayer to take place, thoughts and feelings of which we have been unaware begin to manifest and interrelate. It is as though our psyche knows that it is safe to allow these hidden thoughts and emotions to come into the light. In solitude these deep thoughts are given time to mull, and feelings are felt deeply. This unleashing of what we think and feel in solitude helps to activate our creativity. The freedom to think and feel what comes naturally relieves our tension and promotes our sense of well-being.

Sometimes revelation visits solitude. To leave the crowd and be alone, even for a while, allows the scales from our eyes to fall away, and clears our ears that we may hear. Alone with God, we dream new dreams, and potential is unveiled. In solitude our mind is opened, and our heart is filled with love. What is revealed, what is inspired, is not for us alone. From our solitude in the desert the city will be touched.

*You are the ground of our being, God, the fountain from which our life flows out into the world. Let our being speak your Word. Let our being touch the world for you.*

# Day 3: Leaving the World to Be One with It

*I go away for a while, and I come back to you.*
*(Jn 14:28)*

To seek the solitude our soul requires does not mean that we renounce the world, or that we commit ourselves to the mortification of the flesh or to some form of rigorous discipline. It means that we recognize our need for a solitary life, a life of contemplation and devotion to God alone. It means that in order to truly love the world, we must sometimes leave it for a while. We don't crave solitude because we feel separate from everyone, rather, we want to be in solitude because it is there that we feel one with all creation.

If we seek aloneness as protection against potential pain, if we flee into solitude to escape rejection, then what we will find is loneliness, not solitude. Our solitude must come with the courage to venture into the desert alone, and the courage to live among those whom we love. We can go up the mountain to pray because we have been in the valley with people, and we can be in the valley with people because we have been up the mountain to pray.

*In solitude we see ourselves through your eyes, dear God.*
*There, we respond to the prompting of our truest self.*

# Day 4: Being Alone with God

*An hour is coming – has already come – when you will be scattered and each will go his way, leaving me quite alone. Yet I can never be alone: the Father is with me.* *(Jn 16:32)*

The difference between loneliness and solitude has to do with the awareness of the presence of God. All that is in us and around us is God. God's presence is the ultimate companionship. In our solitude we are alone with God. How can we be lonely?

In solitude we leave all else behind. There is one cause; there is one aim; there is no one but the Beloved. Such is the nature of our solitary heart. In solitude we pray, believing in the unity of all. In purity of heart we realize that we never left the blessed state of our original innocence.

Sometimes we need someone to listen to us for a while and support us emotionally. Sometimes what we need is to be in solitude where we can listen to ourselves and draw support from our deeper selves, and from the God within, who listens to our heart.

*Alone with you, dear God, we are with everyone. In our aloneness is revealed the oneness of All.*

*For everything there is a season, and a time for every matter under heaven: . . . a time to keep silence, and a time to speak; . . .(Ecclesiastes 3:1, 7)*

We are lured into the quiet regions of our soul, and we are drawn toward the stillness of God, but we are afraid of what we do not know. We resist the gentle pull into that deeper part of our reality for fear that we may disappear.

In the silence there are no boundaries, no walls, no fences. Will we lose our way? Where are our bearings? How will we know which way to go? The silence will heal our broken heart, but dare we risk letting go of the noises that we know so well? We are accustomed to making noises in order to know that we are here. We send out sounds to have them bounce back at us and tell us where we are. We fear that silence will leave us lost in the wilderness without a compass and without a clue to who we are.

To enter into the silence we must release our hold on the clamor and the racket, no matter how familiar. We must be willing to deal with our emptiness, and to confront our vulnerability. To enter into silence we must be willing to abdicate our self-sufficiency and to fall back on nothing but the unexpressed.

*As we enter into intimacy with you, dear God, we drop the veil of our imagined self, and reveal the essence of our soul. We come to you with an open, available, and receptive heart.*

# ❊ Day 6: Silencing the Noise Within ❊

*Let all be silent in the presence of the Lord!*
*(Zech 2:13)*

Memories clamor in our mind. We have been deeply injured in body and soul. We may have been abused, betrayed, or abandoned. The noise that comes from what has been will not be silenced by our will. It wants our attention, our understanding, and our compassion. It will not be silenced until we have given it its due, until we have acknowledged our pain and grieved our losses, until we have transcended the past through integration and forgiveness. The noisy memories of our life will not leave us alone; they call us to confrontation; they lead us to reconciliation. Then, and only then, will they surrender to the silence of a healing heart.

Let us be quiet. Let us surrender to the silence of the heart. Here, we will be healed. Here, we will receive the love our soul requires. We can move to shut out the noises of the world around us, but God's peace comes only when we have silenced the noises within us. We discover that our inner silence can be nurtured even in the midst of the external clamor.

*Peace be with us, not the peace of the world, but the peace that is beyond all comprehension; not a peace of calmness, harmony, and tranquility, but a peace that transcends the circumstances of our life.*

# ✤ Day 7: Listening with the Heart ✤

*Be still and know that I am God.*     *(Ps 46:10)*

How wonderful to be alone in the quiet of a meadow. How glorious to view the world below from a solitary place atop a mountain. The silence that surrounds us offers us tranquility. But we don't have to find a meadow; we don't have to climb on high. The silence that our soul requires can be ours no matter where we are. In a crowded airport or on a busy street, our silent heart will give us rest regardless of the noise.

This is our inmost prayer, the silence of the heart. We enter into the silence and we become the silence. Here, we come to accept the reality of the silent love of God. Here, we come to realize that the essence of God's love finds its expression only in the openness of silence. We do not seek peace, yet peace finds us; we do not ask for quiet, yet quiet engulfs us. We are one with God. Here, in the midst of the stillness, we hear the voice of God. It draws us near.

*Silence is the sound of your voice, dear God. It soothes our soul and calms our spirit. Let our response be silent, too.*

You, dear God, are the rainbow in the desert that calls out, "Come, follow me into the heavens. Be at peace. Rest your soul." You are the arch of glorious hues and ephemeral presence that comes at the end of the storm, when You are needed most. The clouds begin to leave and the sunlight filters in. It is now, between a darkened yesterday and a bright tomorrow, that my dream of many colors is born into the world. Just as all seems lost, and despair moves in to reign over my heart, You are there for me to see. You are a strange, mysterious vision that lifts from the depths, and inspires toward the heights. You are the gift divine.

You are the mountain, serene and alluring. You are immense, mysterious, and ever changing, yet faithfully constant. You ascend to the heights of Your heavenly peaks and descend into the depths of Your mystical valleys.

You are the earth, full of love. You nurture me with all that you are, and offer sustenance to me. From Your womb I come and to Your belly I return. In You the roots sink deeply, from You the fruit comes forth, in You I come to rest.

You are the sky, opening and revealing. In You there is no end and no beginning. You hold the stars and offer me infinity. You embrace the cosmos and all that You create. You send the light of life and the dark of death, and they become but one.

*Week III*

# The Wings of the Dawn

*Opening to Love*

*"Where can I go from your spirit? From your presence where can I flee? If I go up to the heavens, you are there; if I sink to the nether world, you are present there. If I take the wings of the dawn, if I settle at the farthest limits of the sea, even there your hand shall guide me, and your right hand hold me fast."* —Psalm 139:7-10

## ❀ Day 1: Forgiving Ourselves and Others ❀

*And when you stand up to pray, forgive whatever you have against anyone, that your Father in heaven may also forgive you your offenses.*

*(Mk 11:25)*

We may carry with us a sense of outrage over wrongs that have been done to us or to others. In the light of contemplation, the shadows disappear and we are granted the freedom of forgiveness. We may come burdened with the heavy load of guilt, but here, in the sweet glow of contemplation, we meet our humble self and embrace all of who we are. It is from this state of humility that the tension of pride and possession is released and our path is redirected. We may come to this place with a broken heart and shattered dream, but through the healing touch of forgiveness we are made whole if only for another day.

We release unto God all that binds us to our lesser selves. God has freed us of all that is held against us, and we can do no less. We pardon the debts owed to us by others, and we forgive ourselves for the error of our ways. God's mercy transcends the justice of the world. God's mercy brings new life where there was death. God's mercy begets our mercy, and our mercy begets God's. All is forgiven in the realm of love.

*God of mercy, you love us so. You ask us to forgive, even as we have been forgiven.*

30

# Day 2: Grieving Our Losses

*. . . you will grieve for a time, but your grief will be
turned into joy.* *(Jn 16:20)*

When we are separated from something or someone we
love, we turn to God. That which we have loved has been torn
from our side, and we are left bleeding, crying, grieving. We
do not want to face the agony of our loss, and we are tempted
to run away. Yet, we dare to stay. We walk through the darkness, believing that we are not alone.

God is with us in the brokenness. God is with us in the desperation. God is with us in the pain. As we commit to our
bereavement, God holds us fast and brings us the comfort that
we need to make it to the other side. Then we are asked to live
in truth. Within the pain, and through the suffering, our energy returns. Our life becomes an offering to the Source from
whence it came.

*The darkness that overcomes us is not victorious, for even
the darkness obeys your light, dear God. We are sustained, we
are encouraged, for we are not alone. You protect our soul and
give us the strength to persevere even when the climb is steep.*

# Day 3: Allowing Joy

*My being proclaims the greatness of the Lord, my spirit finds joy in God my savior.* *(Lk 1:46)*

We are blessed beings. To be blessed means to be consecrated, made sacred or holy; to be worthy of adoration, reverence, or worship; or to be divinely favored. To be blessed also means to be blissfully happy. In others words, to be blessed is to know joy.

Being happy is not the same as being joyful. We can be happy when our lives are going well and suffering is at a minimum. The feeling of happiness comes and goes with the wind of circumstances. But we dare not compare our own contentment or the satisfaction of our needs with the joy that emanates from God. The joy that moves our heart and animates our soul transcends the circumstances of our life, reflecting, instead, the equanimity of our faith.

*Being conscious of your presence, dear God, brings a joy beyond words. All that matters is being with you.*

# Day 4: Searching for Joy

*My heart is restless until it rests in you.*
*(St Augustine)*

Search as we may for true joy, we shall never find it. It eludes us at every turn. Sometimes we focus on that which is missing from our life and attribute to that our lack of joy. We allow our blessedness to be contingent on the state of the external, whether it is health, security, work, or personal relationships. But it is only by embracing our state of lacking that we come to realize that it is God Whom we are lacking in our life, and that nothing short of God can fulfill us.

It is in the letting go of our desire for joy, in the surrendering to reality of that which is, that joy comes into our life. It is not a reward for being faithful, but a consequence of our faith. When we have searched in vain the world over for the treasure of our heart, we come to find that treasure in the heart of God.

*We are willing to suffer in the world for your sake, dear God. Let us also be willing to allow your joy to overtake us.*

## Day 5: Transcending Ourselves

*That is my joy, and it is complete. He must increase, while I must decrease.* *(Jn 3:29, 30)*

We seek fulfillment in life, and yet our soul knows that our only fulfillment comes in union with God. Such union comes, not as a result of our pious will or our strict spiritual discipline, but simply because we become quiet enough, still enough, open enough for the essence of our inner self to emerge. It is this "I" whom we must confront and then transcend as "I" becomes "I Am."

We surrender to God our heart, that God's love may touch the world. We surrender to God our strength that God's work may be done with purpose and vitality. We surrender to God our soul that we may cease and God may live.

*You touch us, God, and we are quickened into consciousness. We touch you and we touch the wounds of the world. Connected to you, love and goodness are our fruit.*

# Day 6: Staying with God

*The Father and I are one.*        *(Jn 10:30)*

In union with God we become detached from everything that separates us from God. We endeavor to be in a constant state of recollection. Our aim is to walk always in the presence of God and never divert our mind from God, but to be recollected in this way is not always possible. However, under every condition, it is possible to love, and this is the essential element. Love is our impetus to pray.

We dare to stay in God's presence. God is part of all we think, all we feel, and all we do. We aspire to live constantly in remembrance of God. We do what we must do, and stay conscious of our union with God at all times. We find God in our heart. We find God in the hearts of others. We find God in all creation. We believe in the immanence of God: God within, God without, God in all that is. Conscious of our connections with God, and aware of God's presence with us, we open to the wisdom that comes.

> *We are in union with you, dear God, when we are in union with all that surrounds us. We find your presence in everything. We know your presence in the face of every person we encounter, and behold your presence in the stars above and the pebbles below.*

## ❁ Day 7: Expressing God in the World ❁

*I ask nothing of you. I don't even ask for your love.*
*I want only you.                    (St Augustine)*

When we acknowledge God's presence within us, we can no longer be passive about what happens in our life. No longer can we just wait to see what God will do with us. God lives through us using our mind, our heart, our strength, and our soul. As we embrace God's presence within us, we take responsibility for our life as co-creators of it.

God's overwhelming love pursues us, no matter where we run in shame, and with it comes the redeeming gift of God's forgiveness. Here is where our soul belongs, here is where God wants us, living in the divine presence every moment of our life. The joy with which God fills us is not for us alone, we must impart it to the world.

*We love you, God, above all else, and our service to you is our purpose in life. To follow you is to leave everything else behind. We are where you are — in the garden of peace and safety, and in the dung pile of trouble and turmoil; on the mountain that touches heaven, and in the pit of grief and sorrow.*

Beloved Being, Source of my spirit, tender of my soul, I love you so. I awaken into your presence, if only for a moment, yet, sufficient to sustain me through the long and lonely night.

I yearn for you, Beloved of my heart, for you are all that is. I hunger for your presence and I thirst for your sweet love. Nothing else can fulfill my one desire.

God of my soul, I live for the moments I can spend with you walking in the garden of my mind. Here, I am one essence with you. Here, I come to know the ecstasy of our communion.

God of Light, you are my focus. You are my mainstay. I look at you with the eyes of my soul and my heart is purified.

*Week IV*

# Blessedness

*Giving Birth To Joy*

*"Blessed are those who dwell in your house, ever singing your praise."* —Psalm 84:4

# Day 1

*Blessed are the poor in spirit, for theirs is the kingdom of heaven.* *(Mt 5:3)*

Blessed be those who accept their poverty and release their illusion of security, power, wealth, or any other treasure to which they cling.

Blessed be those who acknowledge their weakness, and invoke the strength of God; who admit their fear, and receive the courage of God; who declare themselves lost, and take the guiding hand of God. The divine paradox is that when we let go of everything, we have everything. In our emptiness we become a receptacle for the love of God. In our woundedness we are bonded in compassion with a suffering world. In our incompleteness we keep turning back to God.

Blessed be those who free themselves from the illusion of self-sufficiency and are completely reliant on God, for theirs is the joy of trust.

*To be conscious of you, dear God, is to exist in a different state of mind. We have nothing except an intense longing to be touched by you.*

# Day 2

*Blessed are those who mourn, for they will be
comforted.*                                   *(Mt 5:4)*

Blessed be those who have dared to live and love. They
have learned that the other side of life is death, and the other
side of love is loss.

Blessed be those whose loss has moved them to a deeper
place of being. Their joy is born from the pain of giving life, it
ascends from the ashes of their losses. Joy is the fruit of their
sorrow, the rainbow of their storm.

Blessed be those who share their pain and tears of loss with
God, for theirs is the joy of strength.

*Only you, dear God, who mourn with us, can lead us back
to love. Only you, who die with us, can lead us back to life.*

# Day 3

*Blessed are the meek, for they will inherit the earth.* *(Mt 5:5)*

Blessed be those who are grounded in the reality of life just as it is.

Blessed be those who honor their weaknesses as well as their strengths, and realize their limitations as well as their assets.

Blessed be those who release their inordinate ambition to be more than they are, and remember their ephemeral selves.

Blessed be those who dare to come as children, because it is the child within who sees the face of God in everything.

Blessed be those who declare themselves open, available, and receptive to God.

Blessed be those who enter into self-forgetfulness, and go beyond themselves to God, for theirs is the joy of humility.

*Help us, God, to embrace the treasure of our innermost being, and behold our authentic self. Let us dare to be naked, unmasked, and vulnerable, grounded in the reality of who we are.*

41

# Day 4

*Blessed are those who hunger and thirst for right-
eousness, for they will be filled.          (Mt 5:6)*

Blessed be those who know they belong to God, and nothing short of God can fulfill them.

Blessed be those who make God the center of their being,
the purpose of their existence, the focus of their life.

Blessed be those for whom God is the breath by which they
live.

Blessed be those who dare to die that God may live.

Blessed be those who yearn deeply to be one with God, for
theirs is the joy of passion.

*We belong to you, dear God, and nothing short of you can
fulfill us. Inherent in our being is a deep yearning to be one
with you, to be enveloped and sustained by the energy of your
unconditional love.*

*Blessed are the merciful, for they shall be shown mercy.* *(Mt 5:7)*

Blessed be those who accept the forgiveness of God and are willing to pass it on to themselves and others.

Blessed be those who allow their self-righteousness to be turned into tolerance, their indignation into understanding, and their sense of justice into generosity.

Blessed be those who believe in the healing power of mercy, for theirs is the joy of compassion.

*Like the dawning of a new day, dear God, your mercy grants a second chance at life.*

*Blessed are the pure in heart, for they will see God.*                    *(Mt 5:8)*

Blessed be those for whom everything is less important than God.

Blessed be those who seek God with their whole being, and commune with God even through the darkness and the unknowing.

Blessed be those who allow their heart to be real, true, and simple as it rests in God.

Blessed be those who love God with their total self, and surrender their very essence to their Beloved.

Blessed be those who see God in all persons and in all of creation.

Blessed be those who are aware of the immanence of God, for theirs is the joy of consciousness.

*To seek you, God, with our whole being is the instinct of our soul. For this we were born: to remain with you each day in love and devotion.*

# Day 7

*Blessed are the peacemakers, for they will be called children of God.* *(Mt 5:9)*

Blessed be those who are open to a peace, not necessarily of calmness, harmony, and tranquility, but a peace that transcends the circumstances of their life; a peace that is beyond all comprehension.

Blessed be those who believe in the integrating love of God and who offer to the world from the deep, still waters of their soul, for theirs is the joy of oneness.

*Blessed are those who are persecuted for righteousness' sake, for theirs is the kingdom of heaven.*
*(Mt 5:10)*

Blessed be those who love God more than peace itself. Blessed be those who are willing to risk opposition, hostility, and rejection in order to listen to the voice of their heart, and march to the beat of the heavenly drum.

Blessed be those who are willing to lose that which is precious to them, in order to preserve that which is the most precious.

Blessed be those who are willing to sacrifice in the name of love, for theirs is the joy of courage.

*Your healing peace is ours, dear God, even in the midst of the tempest. As we stay true to our belief and live according to your will, Beloved, we may encounter opposition. But whatever suffering may come our way, it cannot touch us at the core where you abide.*

# GOD OF LOVE

God of love, live through me. Let me be your incarnation. Grant that I may be the sign of your holy presence, and reflect unto others the radiance of your light.

God of love, live through me. My eyes are your eyes. Through them you see what you have wrought. My eyes behold the excellence of your creation, large and small. They look with awe upon your heavenly spaces, and they observe with wonder the intricacies of a hummingbird. My eyes gaze at the loveliness of the rose, and delight in the splendor of children playing. My eyes reveal your spirit, they are the windows of your soul.

God of love, live through me. My arms are your arms. They are the arms you use to embrace the sad and broken. They are the arms with which you help the disadvantaged. My arms carry your little ones, and they protect the vulnerable. They work hard toward the betterment of life. My arms are dedicated to you, and are raised in prayer and adoration to all that you are.

God of love, live through me. My mind is your mind. It is used to learn and teach the truth as you reveal it, and it helps you to create a more peaceful world. My mind focuses on that which is important to you. My mind is the channel for your will. Through it I speak to you, and through it I hear your word.

God of love, live though me. My heart is your heart. I feel the sadness and the grief which you feel for the brokenhearted. I am indignant at injustice, and I have compassion for the lost. I feel the joy you feel upon each soul's return. My heart is your heart. I love your every creature, even myself, with the total love that emanates from you.

God of love, live through me. My life is your life.

## Additional Titles Published by Resurrection Press, a Catholic Book Publishing Imprint

| | |
|---|---|
| A Rachel Rosary   *Larry Kupferman* | $4.50 |
| Blessings All Around   *Dolores Leckey* | $8.95 |
| Catholic Is Wonderful   *Mitch Finley* | $4.95 |
| Come, Celebrate Jesus!   *Francis X. Gaeta* | $4.95 |
| Days of Intense Emotion   *Keeler/Moses* | $12.95 |
| From Holy Hour to Happy Hour   *Francis X. Gaeta* | $7.95 |
| Healing through the Mass   *Robert DeGrandis, SSJ* | $9.95 |
| The Healing Rosary   *Mike D.* | $5.95 |
| Healing Your Grief   *Ruthann Williams, OP* | $7.95 |
| Healthy and Holy Under Stress   *Muto, VanKaam* | $3.95 |
| Heart Peace   *Adolfo Quezada* | $9.95 |
| Life, Love and Laughter   *Jim Vlaun* | $7.95 |
| Living Each Day by the Power of Faith   *Barbara Ryan* | $8.95 |
| The Joy of Being an Altar Server   *Joseph Champlin* | $5.95 |
| The Joy of Being a Catechist   *Gloria Durka* | $4.95 |
| The Joy of Being a Eucharistic Minister   *Mitch Finley* | $5.95 |
| The Joy of Marriage Preparation   *McDonough* | $5.95 |
| The Joy of Preaching   *Rod Damico* | $6.95 |
| The Joy of Ushers   *Gretchen Hailer* | $5.95 |
| Lights in the Darkness   *Ave Clark, O.P.* | $8.95 |
| Loving Yourself for God's Sake   *Adolfo Quezada* | $5.95 |
| Mother Teresa   *Eugene Palumbo* | $5.95 |
| Our Grounds for Hope   *Fulton J. Sheen* | $7.95 |
| Personally Speaking   *Jim Lisante* | $8.95 |
| Practicing the Prayer of Presence   *van Kaam/Muto* | $8.95 |
| 5-Minute Miracles   *Linda Schubert* | $4.95 |
| Season of New Beginnings   *Mitch Finley* | $4.95 |
| Season of Promises   *Mitch Finley* | $4.95 |
| Stay with Us   *John Mullin, SJ* | $3.95 |
| Surprising Mary   *Mitch Finley* | $7.95 |
| What He Did for Love   *Francis X. Gaeta* | $5.95 |
| Womansoul   *Pat Duffy* | $7.95 |
| You Are My Beloved   *Mitch Finley* | $10.95 |
| Your Sacred Story   *Robert Lauder* | $6.95 |

For a free catalog call 1-800-892-6657